Is The Interpreter In The House?

Interpreting The Flow Of The Holy Ghost In Your Service

By Virgil L. Stokes

Abundant Heart Ministries
PO Box 90314
Tucson AZ 85752

Abundant Heart Ministries, Inc.
PO Box 90314
Tucson AZ 85752
e-mail: pastorvirgil@abundantheart.org
www.abundantheart.org

Contents

Foreword to the Second Edition

When I first wrote the book which we refer to as "The Interpreter," it was 1996. I was traveling to lots of charismatic churches and seeing many interesting things. We were feeling the ripples of the Toronto Blessing, the Pensacola Revival, and the "holy laughter" movement, and it seemed churches were moving in two opposite directions. Some were rolling in the aisles in every service while others, reacting to perveived excess, pulled back from any type the spiritual manifestation.

As a pastor who had come to love and appreciate the move of the Spirit, I was distressed at what seemed to be a movement toward pseudo-spiritual irrelevance on the one hand and mind-numbing religious deadness on the other. In addition, I found that many pastors were simply frightened by the things of the Spirit. They didn't feel competent to preside in services with surprises. Many had heard the stories of the previous generation of Holy Ghost warriors, but were not confident to step into the flow themselves. I wrote a little manual for these pastors, hoping to help them step out and up. (And, honestly, to help us have a little freedom in our services in their churches.) We were amazed by the response.

Now, ten years later, we are seeing a renewed interest in the book. In the past decade, the divide between "Holy Spirit churches" and those who prohibit or discourage the manifestation of the Spirit has grown wider. Under the banner of becoming "seeker-sensitive," some churches have become Spirit-free instead of Spirit-filled. The theory is that we should order our public services so as not to offend or frighten visitors. The result is that services often become performances for an audience rather than expressions of worship from the family's heart. Sermons are designed to cajole the unbeliever rather than refresh, correct, and equip the Church. We are no longer a "habitation of God through the Spirit."

My reading of scripture leads me to believe that our corporate gatherings are for the purpose of exalting the Lord, repairing broken lives, and preparing the Church for ministry. The most effective and powerful way to accomplish this is to be sensitive and obedient to God the Holy Spirit who will inspire our worship, anoint our preaching, and visit us with manifestations of Himself. There will be explosions of Almightiness. This is supposed to make the unbelieving and ignorant uncomfortable. Unfortunately, it also makes many pastors uncomfortable – there is no recipe to follow, no liturgy to cling to, only a mighty wind, a rushing river, and the threat of wildfire. It certainly risks losing our reputation in the community as respectable religious professionals.

In a day when evil seems to be flooding us, and the problems in people's lives appear more daunting than ever, some honest ministers sense a stirring in their hearts. They want to see people helped. They recognize the futility of their human ability. As they read the New Testament they see the description of a Church full of power and Presence. They are hungry for more than just New Testament doctrine. They want New Testament experience as well. At the end of the day the question is not, "How many came?" so much as "What did they receive?" If the gifts and manifestations of the Spirit are real and given for the profit of all, then we must do whatever is necessary to make room for them. They are the gifts of a God who is good all the time. Every church gathering is an opportunity for God to meet

His people in power. Let us be prepared to cooperate. As we do, we will again come to church with a sense of eager anticipation to see what God will do today.

Chapter 1: Introduction

1 Corinthians 12:31
> *But earnestly desire the best gifts. And yet I show you a more excellent way.*

What a wonderful day! It's Sunday Morning. The sun is bright in a clear blue sky. Everyone is scrubbed and decked. Faces are shining. The church is comfortably full. Familiar faces buoy our sense of belonging. The musicians and singers are in particularly fine form, drawing the congregation into a corporate celebration of the Lord's goodness. As the last worship chorus builds there is a sense of wonder at the felt presence of the glory of God. He is really here!

Then it happens. The music ends. For just a moment ecstasy and expectation charge the atmosphere. Then the silence. First a holy hush. Then an anxious waiting. There is no sound, but we are all aware that minds are whirring. Everyone knows something should happen. As the silence lengthens awe decreases, uneasiness increases. Maybe Sister Shrill will give a tongue. We all hope not.

Finally, mercifully, the Pastor turns on his microphone with an electric thud and welcomes us to Church. He tells us we are blessed to be in the presence of God and bids us shake a few hands and be seated for announcements. We do so with a bittersweet mixture of relief and disappointment.

This scene is quite familiar to most who are Charismatic. For too many it describes their entire worship life. For many pastors it is reminiscent of those services when we have prepared our best, prayed our best, preached our best, then hoped for the best, only to go home with a nagging sense that God had more for the people that day. Some may discuss this with a trusted mentor. Many will suffer with a sense of inadequacy and discouragement. Most will do what they must in order to get to Monday and start over. They have been told this is the norm for pastors.

In recent days many churches and pastors have been experiencing new manifestations of the Spirit or an increase in the flow of things seen occasionally in the past. An oft repeated scenario goes something like this: the Pastor and his wife go to a meeting where they see an outbreak of laughter, weeping, dancing, and other wonderful manifestations of the Spirit. Someone lays hands on them to flow in this anointing. They go home. He preaches on the subject and a few sympathetic parishioners giggle a little. He invites an evangelist to come and bring "this" to his people. The evangelist comes and eventually gets everybody to fall on the floor. Many are genuinely touched by the Lord and excitement reigns. The evangelist leaves after laying hands on the pastor to flow in this anointing.

For a few services the flow continues. Slowly, however, there arises the uncomfortable suspicion that we are doing the same thing over and over. The same people laugh. The same people fall. The tangible awareness of God's presence gives way to an outward act and an inward disappointment. Slowly, services drift back to their old routine. We tell people that God moved that way to stir us up, but He's not moving that way now. Inside we wonder where we went wrong.

If any of this sounds familiar, take heart. You are not alone. I recently had a conversation with a a pastor friend of mine. He had preached in another Church and was somewhat distressed with the service. He knew the pastor there as a genuine man of God, anointed and mightily used by the Holy Spirit, yet in this service the congregation seemed reticent to enter into the supernatural flow of God. They were, as we say, stiff.

My friend was accustomed to being in a church where the move of God is expected and continually fresh, where there is a genuine anticipation in every service to see what God might do today. We both agreed this should be the norm for the New Testament Church. The question he asked echoed the cry birthed in my heart during a summer of itinerant ministry, "Why is it so hard for churches to preach the Word and flow in the supernatural?" It seems the two are often mutually exclusive.

Chapter 2: The Search for the Flow of the Spirit

For a number of years I pastored one of those "Word of Faith" churches where we preached vigorously on faith and healing. I taught the people on the gifts of the Spirit as I had heard them described in Bible School. We experienced some occasional manifestation of prophecy and an occasional tongue and interpretation. In God's infinite mercy, He saved and healed people and added to the Church. Still, I had a sense of dissatisfaction in my spirit.

While I was in Tulsa attending a meeting, the Lord spoke to me concerning the supernatural in our services. As I meditated on 1 Corinthians 2:1-5, He told me to start having "Spirit and Power Meetings" on Sunday evenings. In these meetings we would have no program. We would wait on the Lord and worship Him. We would practice following the leading of the Holy Spirit in the service. During two years of these services we got a real education in the flowing with the Spirit of God.

During this period I was reading all I could find on the subject of flowing with Holy Ghost and supernatural ministry. One book by Kenneth E. Hagin, Learning to Flow with the Spirit of God, contained this gem of wisdom in discussing the gift of interpretation: "That is what I do in a lot of our services. I interpret which way the service is going. I think there is a great deal more to 'interpretation' than what we have seen." It dawned on me that God was teaching me the ministry of interpretation in our Sunday night services.

From the beginning of my pastoral ministry I have been used in interpretation of tongues. While in Bible school I heard Lester Sumrall say that the interpretation of tongues was a gift every pastor must have. When I received a call to pastor I told the Lord He would have to provide that gift or I would not be properly equipped. From that day to this I have always had the interpretation of any tongue given in a service where I was in charge. I am even so bold as to tell people they can give a tongue with confidence because they know an interpreter is present. First Corinthians 14:28 says to refrain from giving a tongue as a public utterance when there is no interpreter present.

1 Corinthians 14:27-28:

27 If any man speak in an unknown tongue, let it be by two, or at the most by three, and that by course; and let one interpret.

28 But if there be no interpreter, let him keep silence in the church; and let him speak to himself, and to God. (KJV)

Interpretation has always been understood to mean that if someone speaks aloud in an unknown tongue, someone else must tell the rest of us what God is saying. This means the interpreter will give a sort of "prophecy lite." In other words, one will speak with tongues, and the other will receive inspired utterance that gives the sense of the statement. First Corinthians 14:15 lets us know that tongues and interpretation is equivalent in stature to prophecy for the edification of the church.

This understanding of interpretation is a good one. We have all seen this in manifestation when it has brought great blessing to the service. A pastor would do well to seek this gift earnestly. It is invaluable to a person regularly in charge of public services. I believe, however, that Brother Hagin's comment about the interpreter gives us a clue to a broader understanding of interpretation.

Chapter 3: Expanding the Scope of Interpretation

Look back at 1 Corinthians 14:28, *"But if there be no interpreter, let him keep silence in the church...."* It seems to me that what we actually practice in most churches is a far cry from what is intended in this verse. We tell people not to give a tongue without an interpreter. Most believers are honest and want to please the Lord. When they sense the Spirit moving on them to give an utterance in tongues, they often fail to give it for fear that there is no interpreter. They have no idea if an interpreter is present and don't want to be disobedient.

In our genuine attempts to practice this verse, we have essentially suppressed the flow of God. Sometimes we tell folks that if there is no interpreter they should pray and get the interpretation themselves based on verse 13 of the same chapter. Unfortunately, this is beyond the faith of most; so they clam up. At other times we imply, or explicitly teach, that if someone gives a tongue and there is no interpretation, then the tongue was not of God. This is not necessarily true. The verse says, *"if there is no interpreter...."* The problem is in the lack of an interpreter, or the lack of information about who might be an interpreter, not in the tongue. We have established a rule that has served to keep us comfortable, and keep the Spirit quiet. It allows us to blame the speaker any time no interpretation comes forth rather than seeking for God to flow in interpretation.

If we could be honest, our usual practice is to wait for some brave soul to finally overcome all his fear and speak out in a tongue. Then we all wait with bated breath to see if it was God. If someone interprets, it was God. If not, then we all get uncomfortable and look at our shoes, waiting to see if Pastor is going to correct the offender. The verse does not say to blurt out a tongue and hope God gives someone the interpretation. Quite to the contrary, Paul's implication is that the people in Corinth had certain individuals in their congregation who were recognized as interpreters. If a person had a tongue he could look around and determine if an interpreter was present. All the regulars knew who they were. It was common knowledge. This was a recognized gift!

The words "interpret" and "interpretation" come from the Greek word diermeneuo. This can mean to translate, interpret, expound or explain thoroughly. I particularly like the last definition. We could call this "the Gift of Explanation," and those so gifted could be called "Explainers." The Complete Biblical Library Greek-English Dictionary says this word means, "taking the unintelligible and making it understandable." This would certainly include what we have always referred to as "interpretation," but it could cover so much more.

Look with me at 1 Corinthians 14, verse 23.

> *Therefore if the whole church comes together in one*
> *place, and all speak with tongues, and there come*
> *in those who are uninformed or unbelievers, will*
> *they not say that you are out of your mind?*

Notice our interpretation or explanation is directed at two classes of people: the unbeliever and the uninformed or ignorant. When we reach those places in the service, whether during prayer time or worship, when all are speaking in tongues, we need to explain. We are not required to tell them what is being said, but we can tell them what is going on. If we don't, we have a Bible promise that they will think we are crazy. That is exactly what most of the world and much of Christendom believe about us because we have not explained.

Now notice the same chapter in verses 5 and 6:

5   *I wish you all spoke with tongues, but even more that you prophesied; for he who prophesies is greater than he who speaks with tongues, unless indeed he interprets, that the church may receive edification.*

6   *But now, brethren, if I come to you speaking with tongues, what shall I profit you unless I speak to you either by revelation, by knowledge, by prophesying, or by teaching?*

I was taught, and have dutifully practiced, the precept that tongues plus interpretation is equal to prophecy. In light of verse 5, I believe that to be true. But for years I didn't see verse 6. It says that an interpretation, or an explanation, may be in the form of a revelation, knowledge, prophesying, or teaching. In other words, when the Spirit is speaking in and through His people by using other tongues, there are a number of ways an interpreter or explainer can give the sense of what God is doing and saying. The whole argument of Chapter 14 is not tongues versus prophecy, but intelligibility versus unintelligibility. The Explainer is one who helps us understand.

This accounts for an experience I have had on several occasions. While visiting another church or meeting, a tongue will come forth. I have in my spirit the sense of what God is saying, but there is no unction to give the interpretation. (If you're a stranger in a place, it is often best to hold your peace unless God supernaturally opens the door.) Then someone gives an interpretation that doesn't seem to fit or is only a partial unfolding. Later, when the pastor gets up to preach he will get off on a side track that covers the ground I had in my spirit. This is God using him in the Gift of Explanation in the form of a teaching. Most of the time the pastor is unaware this has happened.

It is entirely possible that the list in verse 6, "by revelation, by knowledge, by prophesying, or by teaching," is not exhaustive, but exemplary. That is, Paul is not giving us a list of all the ways interpretation may be manifested. Instead, there are infinite possibilities. We know from verse 15 of the same chapter that interpretation may take the form of a song. Is this not a manifestation of spiritual songs as described in Colossians 3:16? The Greek word for interpretation is used in Luke 24:27 to describe what Jesus did when He expounded from the Old Testament. Could interpretation include scriptural exegesis, or simply the reading of a specific passage at a specific time?

I have come to believe that the Gift of Interpretation, as practiced by one who can be called an Interpreter, can cover a broad list of things. It can be an interpretation of a tongue in the usual sense. It can be a spiritual song. It can be a teaching to explain the manifestations in a service.

The Gift of Interpretation, or Explanation, can include anything that takes the unintelligible and makes it understandable. This includes discerning the flow of the Spirit in a service and moving the service in that direction. The Explainer is set in the church by God to make sense of what is happening in a service for the benefit of any who might be uninformed or unbelievers.

The answer to my friend's question about why some churches have such a hard time moving in the supernatural is often this simple: They have no Explainer. People will flow where they are comfortable and informed. If their pastor is sensitive to the flow of the Spirit and keeps them informed about what is happening, they will be ready to move. If, however, he is slow to follow the Holy Ghost or does not explain to them what is happening, they will be stubborn, frightened, and skeptical. Notice, he may be mightily used in gifts of the Spirit, but without explanation there will be no consistent flow in the body.

The main ingredient for a supernatural church is a pastor who flows in the Gift of Explanation. If you are called to pastor, I believe you can step out in faith by asking God for this gift. He said to desire the best ones, and this is one you need. If this idea is new to you, it may take a while to get comfortable in the flow. When we sense the anointing, most of us automatically revert to what we know and do best. I am a teacher. The natural, comfortable thing for me is to teach. I have often killed the service by starting to teach only to have the anointing lift almost immediately. I've had to learn to leave my comfort zone and broaden my spiritual outlook. God has an infinite variety of ideas for church service.

As I have begun to recognize this gift and watch for its operation, I have seen that most of the ministers who are having great manifestation of the Spirit in their meetings are actually functioning as Explainers. They constantly tell people what is happening and frequently encourage others to be involved in the service. I see this same thing in churches where the supernatural continues on any regular basis. The pastor, or someone he trusts and uses, keeps the congregation informed. The unintelligible is made understandable.

God has a grand plan for every gathering of the saints. Verse 26 of 1 Corinthians 14 indicates that every person comes to the service with something that might be a blessing:

> *How is it brethren? Whenever you come together,*
> *each of you has a psalm, has a teaching, has a*
> *tongue, has a revelation, has an interpretation. Let*
> *all things be done for edification.*

God wants us to bring out the things that will be the greatest help in accomplishing His plan for that particular service. The Explainer is like the baton in the hand of the conductor. The eyes of the orchestra are on the baton waiting for its movements to convey to them the pace and direction of the music. You are in the hand of the Spirit, the Conductor of every service. He moves you, and the congregation flows in unison with the rhythm of the Spirit.

Chapter 4: Flowing in the Gift of Explanation

There are a number of churches flowing in the supernatural and in the truth of God's Word today. Praise God for them. If you are in one of those places you should fall on your knees and thank the Lord. In Pentecostal and Charismatic circles there have always been churches where there is much emotional activity, which may or may not be supernatural, but it is accompanied by precious little sound doctrine. As a result of the great teaching revival of the seventies and eighties, there are now many churches with excellent and accurate teaching of the Bible, many of whom have little or no manifestation of the supernatural. I found myself in this latter category until I began to learn how to be an Explainer.

The first step in flowing with the Spirit in your service is to realize that you currently don't. Many good "Word" pastors simply "harrumph" at the suggestion that God is not moving as He wants. They say things like, "We need to get back to basics," or "The Word is where people get their help. We have to emphasize the Word." While these things are true as far as they go, they also may be used as rationalization for the nagging sense that God has more and we are missing it. Remember, if we preach Bible doctrine we ought to have Bible experience.

In determining the condition of your church you have to be honest. Is your service as predictable as the denomination down the street? Can people plan their late entry because they know exactly when the singing ends? How often do things happen in your services that you feel need to be explained to visitors? Do you or anyone else in your congregation have a genuine sense of anticipation before services? Have you done your absolute best but still have a gnawing suspicion that there must be more? Do you get defensive when you read questions like these?

If you don't like your answers to these questions then there are a few things you can do. Don't feel lonesome. You're not alone. I have spoken to pastor after pastor who feels he is a good teacher, counselor, or administrator but senses a woeful inadequacy in the things of the Spirit. This sense of discomfort usually leads to an avoidance of the issue. Some even attempt to avoid the supernatural in services because they don't feel equipped to handle it. Many of us have been brought up on stories of how things happened so marvelously years ago, but we have had very little instruction or example in how to flow in these things ourselves. It's time we pressed in.

Chapter 5: Step Up and Receive Your Mantle

If God has called you to pastor or otherwise regularly lead services then you must accept that responsibility. When you are in charge of the service, God has delegated to you the authority to direct that gathering. Don't be bashful, ashamed, or falsely humble. Surely you don't want to be controlling or overbearing, but you do want to contend for the flow of God. He has placed you in the driver's seat for that particular service.

I want to impress upon you a spiritual law: Someone will control every service. If it is not you it will be someone else. If the person God put there to explain and interpret does not fill that role, the sheep will find someone else to follow. The direction of the service will depend on who steps into that driver's seat. There may be wildfire, there may be no fire, there may be strange fire, but it is sure fire that you will have nothing to say about it. Unfortunately, it is you who will have to answer for it when Jesus inspects His church.

One place many pastors get off track is in delegating away all control of the music ministry. I don't mean to say you have to be a musician or lead the worship, but the pastor is responsible for the whole service, not just the sermon. Music is not an afterthought or part of the so-called "preliminaries." It is, in fact, a primary component in the flow of God.

In most churches the service is compartmentalized into the singing and the Word, separated by the announcements. Many pastors are not comfortable in "tampering" with the music, yet they are actually responsible for it. The worship service starts when the music begins and it ends with the benediction. There is no partition, only a flow from one phase to another as crafted by the Holy Ghost.

Don't be afraid to express your ideas about the music. If you sense the Spirit moving in a particular song, find a way to communicate to your worship leader to camp out on that one. Never leave a song while God is visiting His people in it. If the service reached a certain place of intensity and you sense the unction to minister, move to the pulpit and flow right into ministry. The song list is a tool, not a law.

Be sure to know the last song planned and move to the pulpit while the singing continues. It is particularly helpful for the pastor to join in on the last song. Let the next part of the service flow straight from the presence of God. If there was one song in the service that was particularly blessed that day, go back to it and end the singing on that note of anointing.

If you have favorite songs that assist you in getting in the Spirit, be sure you communicate them to your worship leader. By the same token, feel free to eliminate songs you particularly dislike. I endured one particular chorus for years because I didn't want to seem unspiritual or offend my music department. Every time that silly chorus started I felt my insides cringe. I tried to appear joyful, but it only made me angry. I finally told the music team to stop using it. They did so without a murmur. What a relief!

Taking control of the music is one aspect of stepping up to take the steering wheel for the whole service. Another vital aspect is exercising your responsibility to deal with outbursts and disturbances that are not of God. Many pastors are very uncomfortable with this. Most simply don't feel confident enough in the things of the Spirit to believe they know what to do. Some are afraid they will offend. I promise, people will be grateful. There is a sense of security that comes with the knowledge that someone is taking responsibility.

The methods of correction are many and varied. I always use this rule of thumb: If it causes fear or confusion, deal with it now, in front of all. If a babe in Christ bursts forth with a flesh prophecy, I might opt to correct him privately after the service. If, however, he says or does something that is doctrinally incorrect or that leaves a sense of distress in the service, I will tell him right then. Every flesh outburst does not need to be corrected, but only those that may lead to difficulties. The gift of the Explainer will help you discern. Things that are clearly not God can offer wonderful opportunities to explain the operation of the Spirit. Correction becomes instruction.

When God begins to move, people will react in many different ways. Most people respond to the presence of God in the manner they saw when they first came into the kingdom or in the way currently popular in the church world. Some people get very quiet. Some shake. Some weep. Some fall or weave or laugh. Some Charismatics think they have to prophesy and will blurt out something just to fill the silence. Whatever goes on, some will be flesh and some will be Spirit.

If there are those present who may not understand, the Explainer needs to explain what is happening. "Brother Breakdown is shaking under the power of God. You might react to the touch of God differently and that is OK." Many problems can be avoided by simply letting people know that everything is all right and somebody knows what's happening. One manifestation that always demands explanation is laughter. Outsiders will often think we are being sacrilegious. **The Explainer must explain.**

Some of the things we become accustomed to are still quite bizarre to the uninitiated. Remember the first time you saw someone raise their hands to worship? I remember one young man new to our church who came into the prayer line for healing. As I proceeded down the line toward him, each person dutifully stiffened and fell into the catchers waiting arms. After I laid hands on our young visitor, he looked around, noted the appropriate behavior, and carefully laid down on the floor next to my previous victim. He thought this was part of our liturgy.

Explain, explain, explain!

Chapter 6: Exercise a Little Faith

If you believe God has placed you in charge of a service, then you need to trust Him to give you direction in that service. As a pastor who needs the gift to do his job, you can pray for the Gift of Explanation to be manifest in your ministry, then simply begin to thank Him for it. As a step of faith, you might teach on the subject and tell your congregation you are learning to flow as an Explainer. (If you have convinced them you are perfect and already know everything, ask them to forgive you for lying.) Tell them they can safely step out to give a tongue if you are present, because you are an Explainer.

Probably the most useful thing I did to learn the touch of the Spirit was designate a service for that purpose. Our Sunday evenings were announced as Holy Spirit services. People were instructed that we were all learning and would all miss it, but we could learn from our mistakes. I did no preparation for this service other than to pray in the Spirit for an hour prior. Sometimes God would give me a scripture or a theme during this time. Other times He would say nothing.

The service consisted of worship and obedience. We started with worship. In this kind of service keep it simple and flexible. I play guitar, so usually I just sat and began a chord progression. If you have no musicians for such a task, you can do it *a capella*. You could even play a favorite tape to get the service started. It is important to get delivered from the popular notion that God can't move without professional musicians. He inhabits the praises of His people, not the blank stares of an audience.

One benefit we experienced was a fresh sense that we are not bound to modern technology. For many Americans, it is not worship without reverb, surround sound, and laser lights. Face it, friends, that is flesh. I love my amplifier and effects pedal as much as the next guy, but some of the most powerful visitations of God I have ever seen have happened with no instruments or microphones. It is entirely possible to have a worship service without electricity. In fact, some people desperately need to hear themselves worship. They have never had the experience. Many a congregation could benefit from hearing the holy symphony created by the God-given voices of the saints in worship.

In our Holy Ghost services we determined to worship the Lord until He directed us differently. Sometimes we just sang for 90 minutes and went home. That was OK. Sometimes He moved on someone else. Usually there came an idea that seemed pristine clear or at least persistent: "Have people give testimony." "Let people share what the Lord has been teaching them this week." "Ask if anyone has a word from God." "Each one read your favorite scripture." "Who has a song on their mind?" The list is endless. The point is, if I believe God has anointed me as Explainer in this service, I need to pay attention to the thoughts He places in my heart and act on them. This is how I learn to discern.

It is an absolutely normal and natural human tendency to repeat anything that is enjoyable or effective. We have even pro-verbialized this concept in the phrase, "If it's not broke, don't fix it." This is not always wisdom. It can prevent us from moving from good to better to best. We have to be careful not to look for the same manifestation in every service or to repeat the formula that brought great blessing last time. God is infinitely creative. Be available to try a new direction. Admit when the blessing has moved and get busy moving with it.

As an act of my faith that God has given me grace to interpret the service, I have found it useful to ask that people be recognized from the platform before operating any gift of the Spirit. They simply raise their hand and I recognize them if it bears witness with my spirit. If I have no sense of warning or distress in my heart, then I assume it is OK with God. If the timing does not seem right, I ask that they hold it until later. If I fail to recognize them and we miss the will of God then the guilt is mine. They have been obedient and submissive. This requires me to stretch my faith and it provides the congregation with the sense of security that comes with knowing that someone is at the helm.

Another simple method of developing faith to follow the Spirit is by preaching without notes. I am a stickler for preparation and organization in presentation, but we might as well face it, dry is dry no matter how well organized. Many of us who came up in the teaching tradition are tied to our notebook. We will benefit by getting free. Second Corinthians 3:1-3 indicates that God writes letters on our hearts by the Holy Spirit. Take a leap of faith by spending time in prayer and study, then throw away your paper and read God's epistle off the tablet of your heart. If He wanted to write a fresh letter to your congregation, that is exactly where He would write it. The result might surprise you.

Chapter 7: Learn To Wait

The key to a fresh flow of the Spirit in our services turned out to be very simple. I had to get humble enough to wait on the Lord and then obey Him right there on Sunday morning in front of God and everybody. Like most pastors, I came to every service with an idea of what was going to happen. I had a carefully prepared message, often part of a series that the world desperately needed to hear and have on tape. Our song service and children's ministries and announcement-maker and refreshment server and usher corp and prayer counselor team and ad nauseam were all carefully coordinated. Besides, we have to be seeker-sensitive, don't we? We wouldn't want any outsiders to be bothered with the presence of God.

The pressure to move swiftly from one part of the service to the next is great. We are an MTV society. Silence is no longer peaceful, it is uncomfortable. In the face of all the pressures to be organized and efficient, the Lord gave me His advice, "Now learn to wait on Me in your Sunday morning service." I had visions of kneeling and praying in tongues for an hour in front of a full sanctuary while all the sheep thought of how ignorant I was. This Holy Ghost thing is all right on Sunday night, but Sunday morning is the big show. Pride is a terrible taskmaster, almost as powerful as habit. Neither one should control our worship.

With considerable fear and trembling, I announced to our congregation that I was going to attempt to learn to follow God more closely in our service. To my great amazement they were thrilled. In actual practice, we simply learned to take time in the service to be quiet and pray until I had a sense of God's direction. I learned it was OK to tell people, "Let's pray in the Spirit for a moment." They felt a part of a corporate endeavor as we took time to listen to God.

As part of the ministry of Explanation, I informed them regularly that I might be worshiping or praying in tongues while waiting on God. I explained that this use of tongues did not need to be interpreted because I was not speaking to them, I was speaking to God. They could, in fact, join with me as we sought His face. You can never explain too many times or too simply.

Some pastors and many parishioners immediately get nervous and ask, "Isn't this going to make our services too long?" My experience showed that most services were about the same length. The time spent listening to God was more than atoned for in the reality that when we do it His way it goes faster. He can do more in three seconds of anointing than I can do in three days of dead, dry teaching and counseling. We've all been in one hour services that seemed eternal and three hour services that went by in a moment. I found that most people didn't want to leave when the service was over. It was a refreshing change from surreptitious glances at the watch followed by the noon sprint to the parking lot.

Having decided to take the risk of waiting on God in public, the next challenge was to learn what I was waiting for. Several years ago I heard Norvel Hayes say, "God moves according to atmospheres." In any service, there is an atmosphere charged with some aspect of the person of our God. If we can discern this we can flow with Him. When I wait on God I first simply check in my spirit to test the atmosphere.

There are atmospheres of healing, atmospheres of praise, atmospheres of repentance, atmospheres of joy, or there may be a flow from one to another. The possibilities are as infinite as our God. When the presence of God is in the service in a particular way, don't be afraid to camp out. You don't have to move on. God told Israel that when the cloud moves, you move, but not until. Don't move by the clock, or the program, or your pride.

Move with the cloud.

I recall one service where we had a visiting minister. He talked about love. Suddenly the presence of God came in the room in a tangible way. This minister had the good sense to sit down and shut up. My temptation was to pray the benediction or give an altar call. Instead, we all sat in the presence of Love in total silence for about twenty minutes. Then, without a word, people began going to one another and hugging. Rebellious teenagers asked forgiveness from parents. Homes were restored. It was powerful. **The lesson to be learned is simple but not easy. We must not move until God does.**

The other side of the same coin is also simple. If you lose the flow, stop and get back in it. This one is difficult because it means risking the possibility that people will think you have made a mistake. Perish the thought! Surely you all know the feeling. The service is going so well. I am preaching along when suddenly that unction lifts and I feel like I am running through deep mud. That is the time to stop and say, "Let's wait on God." Often, the congregation will get back in God-focus and the anointing will return. At other times you can reflect a moment, remember where you were when the anointing lifted, and go back to that track.

I was recently in Haiti teaching a pastor's seminar. Most of the participants were from non-Pentecostal denominations. I had the dubious honor of instructing them on divine healing. For three days I watched the looks of consternation on their faces as I told them of the will of God to heal. I knew they loved me. It was clear they wanted to believe. But I was teaching them things they had been warned against. By popular demand, a question and answer session was scheduled the last day of the seminar.

Anticipating a lively debate (translate that "strife"), I asked the Lord for His help in my final teaching session before the questions. He impressed me to serve Communion and teach on the power in His broken body. By the time the questioning was to begin, the room was filled with the presence of the Lord and pastors were kneeling and weeping at His feet. Instead of debate we had glory. The atmosphere shifted from contention to awe. Jesus confirmed to those present His endorsement of what was taught. God overcame the program. I simply knelt to worship with the rest and the Lord took care of the questions.

Remember, no matter how spiritual your activity, it is useless without the anointing of the Holy Spirit. Christianity is supernatural. God wishes to be supernaturally involved with our services. Whether it's during the worship time, in the middle of your sermon, while serving communion, during the announcements or the offering, God may want to break in with His power and presence. He is, however, a gentleman and will not intrude on our self-driven party. Take time to invite Him, acknowledge Him, and listen to Him.

Chapter 8: Learn To Play Your Instruments

If you will, allow me to return to the metaphor of the conductor's baton. The Holy Spirit is the Conductor of the Symphony. You are striving to flow with the Conductor to direct the interplay, the rhythm, and the relative volume of the instruments. The instruments are the people in your congregation. The Spirit of God places gifts in them and anoints those gifts. He then uses the Explainer to point out what instrument needs to come to the forefront at any given time of the concert.

Our first job is to lay aside the need to be in the spotlight. In reality, the Explainer who does his job well will be little noticed. No one leaves the symphony applauding the baton. It is vital to recognize that every person in your congregation could give forth something from the Lord that would bless the service. Some instruments are better tuned than others, some musicians more experienced. One instrument may better fit a certain type of music, but each has a note to play.

This is the essence of 1 Corinthians 14:26:

> *How is it then, brethren? Whenever you come together, each of you has a psalm, has a teaching, has a tongue, has a revelation, has an interpretation. Let all things be done for edification.*

Everybody has something. The question is, what does the Conductor think will go best at this moment, a bassoon or a timpani?

As an Explainer, I found that God would sometimes point me to specific people. He does this in different ways and for different purposes. He may want to minister to that person individually. He may want to use that person in some manner to bless the service. If I sense a drawing to a particular person, I call them out and pray for them. Sometimes that is all that happens. Other times, there is a special need that requires ministry. If there are others with the same need, a time of prayer can ensue. At times, gifts of the Spirit will manifest as hands are laid on the individual.

I know the question comes to some, "How does God draw you to a specific person?" If you are like me, you are looking for a burning bush. God is usually more subtle. Most often He uses the same method He used to move Jesus to minister to the crowd in Mark 6:34. He will pour out in your heart a thimble of His compassion. If you sense this special love toward some individual or group, don't hesitate to act on it. Pray for them. Let Jesus love them. This is God demonstrating His nature in the service.

Have you ever preached a message and found yourself repeatedly looking at or walking toward one or two individuals? This could be the Lord wanting you to minister to that person. I found that when I had this kind of drawing to someone I should call them out and pray for them. If nothing else happens, that's fine. Prayer is a blessing. But often this is the beginning of a sequence or episode of ministry. The Spirit begins to flow in wonderful ways.

One Sunday morning we had several visitors from a local home for boys. There was one young man way in the back of the room who just kept catching my eye. All during my sermon I was drawn to him. He didn't stand out in the natural, but I just kept looking back to him. Finally, I walked all the way to the back, laid my hand on his shoulder, and said something. I don't even remember what I said. As it turns out, that young man was unsaved and was being courted by the Muslims. He had prayed on the way to church. He told God that if Jesus was real He should have the preacher come and lay his hand on him. Never discount those gentle promptings!

As I learned to wait on the Lord, I also learned to watch my flock. I found that I could often see the effects of the Spirit moving on them. Some folks start to shake when they sense the power. One dear saint would yawn when she sensed the touch of the Holy Spirit. I have known several folks who begin to flush and turn red. One of my men who often was used to give a tongue would flush and begin to perspire. As carnal as this sounds, learning to watch for these things is significant. The Lord may want to minister to these particular people either individually or in a group. He may want to use that person in some gift and they need you to encourage them to step out. Use observation, coupled with the witness in your spirit and you will see a greater move of God. It is OK to ask them, "What is the Lord doing?" or "God's touching you, isn't He?"

The Lord used this type of cue to set one of my men free to dance in the Spirit. This gentleman was one of my board members. He was a great guy, but rather quiet. A large, muscular man, he was not given to lavish expression. During worship one Sunday I noticed his feet moving in a sort of hop-shuffle. Inwardly I asked the Lord about this unusual behavior. I suddenly felt an unction to speak to him. I just had this sudden, very clear idea of what I should say to him. While the music continued, I stepped to the edge of the platform, pointed to him and said, "John, if you will yield to that, you will dance in the Spirit." He took two steps forward and then broke into one of those uncoordinated, free-form dances of unmitigated joy that only the Spirit of God can produce. He has been dancing ever since.

There is a step in the Spirit that goes beyond looking for the natural effects of the anointing. As you move in the Gift of Explanation the Lord may bless you with supernatural cues to highlight certain people. Several years ago He told me to "pray for the people who light up." From that time I have noticed people in services who begin to glow. This is not visible to others, nor can those persons sense it. I have found that, while I can't make it happen, I must be careful to avoid overlooking it or rushing past it. I must remember to look for it. Perhaps God will bless you with a supernatural highlighter of some kind. It can't hurt to ask.

Learn who plays what instrument. They are tools for the Spirit of God to use in enhancing the song He is playing. If you are going to conduct a symphony, it is good to know who plays what instrument. In every congregation there are those gifted to be used regularly in special ways. In your congregation there are those with the gift of diverse tongues. There are those who can prophesy with regularity. There are others with specific gifts of healings. Some have the gift of exhortation. Some can sing under the Spirit's unction. Be sensitive to these people and learn to recognize them. They are tools for the Spirit of God to use in enhancing the song He is playing.

If you know people in your congregation who are gifted in specific ways, talk to them outside the service. Let them know you want to use them. Learn to identify when they have some-thing, then check on the inside to see if it is the time. Usually, I assume that if God doesn't want me to acknowledge someone He will give me that little sense of drawing back on the inside. If

I don't have a sense that He is saying "NO," I normally go ahead and recognize the person.

As the Spirit prompts, take opportunity to use these people as examples to the congregation. You will only see manifestation of the gifts in your church to the extent that you explain their nature and give opportunity for their exercise. Most people in our country are in a spectator frame of mind when they come to church. Their expectation is that you will have a spiritual experience and tell them about it. That is not Christianity. Your job is to explain to them what they can expect and how to recognize when God is trying to use them. New information brings new expectation.

Through being around my wife I learned to be alert for the healing anointing. She has a hand that begins to burn when it is time to pray for the sick. I did a little polling of my congregation and discovered there were several who had similar experiences. As I began to recognize these gifts and use them to minister to the sick, we improved our results markedly. We also found more people who were gifted in this way but had never known what it was. Get over the idea that you are the only person God can use in your church. Tap into all the resources available. I wonder how much more effective we could be if we actually mobilized what God has given us.

Chapter 9: Learn From Your Mistakes

Thank God for His mercy. He has made the church so strong and His people so loving that they keep coming back even though pastors are imperfect. They endure through our mistakes. Those awful services that left me joyless or even sort of sickened are the ones from which I gleaned the most. I could often look back and see where we missed it and try to be alert to that pitfall in the future. We need to begin to keep our eyes open and study the ways of God in our own ministry. When you have an unfulfilling service, don't just mourn, learn.

One of the biggest lessons to learn is when to quit preaching. I remember one minister saying it was important to quit when you're through. True! Even better, we should learn to quit when God is through. The most frequent mistake I made for years was preaching in the flesh after the anointing had lifted. It is hard work and does little good. I always felt terribly exhausted after those services. Unfortunately, like most preachers, I was enamored of my own voice and assumed everyone else was.

It was important for me to look back at the service in honesty and see where I lost it. Usually, there was one clear point God was trying to make in the message. He did not feel compelled to teach the people everything I thought I knew. Instead of sensing the urgency of the Spirit in the specific area He wanted to emphasize, I would become concerned that I wasn't going to finish my sermon. I would rush on to the next point at the expense of moving away from the anointing.

In analyzing my mistakes, it was very helpful to think about why I kept my own agenda instead of following God's. The primary reasons were ignorance and tradition. I was quite ignorant about the way of the Spirit. I thought the only spiritual way to have a service was the way it was done in the churches I attended. We sing six songs. We sing in tongues. We announce. We pay. We preach. We pray. We go home. The message lasts one hour. The prayer line is at the end of the service at the front of the sanctuary. And so on.

God had to help me see where I was bowing to tradition. Jesus said that traditions of men make the Word of no effect (Mark 7:13). If you are wondering why the Word is not bearing the fruit you think it should in your church, this is a good place to start an investigation. First, I had to learn the definition of a tradition. A tradition of men is anything I do because I saw someone else do it or because that's the way we did it last time and it worked.

I found I had some really stupid ideas. One idea that had to go was the notion that ministry only takes place at the end of the service. It belongs there if it is associated with acting on what has been preached, that is, sermon-related ministry. If I teach on healing, I should pray for the sick at the end. A teaching on marriage should be followed by ministry to marriages. People need an opportunity to act on what they have just heard. But be aware that God may want to move by His Spirit any time during the service as a sign or a confirmation. He may not want the sick to wait two hours to get healed. He may love them more than that!

There are many other places we fall into tradition. Why do we meet on Wednesday night? Why do we stretch our hands out toward people being prayed for? Why do we line people up and hit them in the forehead to heal their illnesses? Why do we serve communion once a month (or whenever)? Why do we do water baptisms at an ancillary service? The important thing is to become aware of what we do and ask the question: "Is it God or is it tradition?" In order to be an **Explainer, you first have to ask questions.**

Another reason I found that I missed the flow of the Spirit was people-pleasing. I didn't like to admit that, but it was true. Sometimes I just didn't want to do anything to upset anybody. Other times, I was afraid I would miss God and appear foolish. As soon as I started holding back from following God because of what people would think, the service was over. We usually continued for an hour or so, but the service ended when I placed my pride first.

I have found that people are much less likely to be offended by the move of the Spirit if there is an Explainer present. Since I recognized my responsibility and gift in that ministry, the manifestation of the Spirit has increased and the offenses have decreased. Most people get offended by what they don't understand. Lack of knowledge produces fear and fear produces loathing. The ministry of the Explainer eliminates many problems, especially for the uninformed and the unbeliever.

Most of us have been brought up in ministry with heroes of faith. We read their books, attend their services, and mimic their methods. This is normal. It is important, however, to recognize that we have gifts that are our own. We each have to learn to flow in our own anointing. This requires being open and obedient, then being alert to see patterns in the flow of the Spirit in our own ministry. These things need to be explained to the people when we minister. It helps them to receive if they know why we do what we do.

When we first noticed that God was anointing my wife's right hand to pray for the sick, I started using her in prayer lines. I would send her one way and I would go the other. One Sunday we met in the middle of that line. I had my hands on a young lady when Judy walked up behind me and laid her hot hand on my back. There was an immediate surge of power running out of her hand and through my arms. The young lady was knocked back into the front row by the power of God.

Not being one to get in the way of the Lord, I sent Judy to pray for the rest of the people in the line. As any good basketball coach will tell you, get the ball to the player with the hot hand! When she prayed by herself, there was no unusual manifestation. We experimented with this phenomenon over several weeks and found that there were certain times when God wanted to use us together. It seemed to work best when I laid hands on the individual and Judy put her hand on my back. This was odd, but it worked. It worked best when I explained it to the people before we ministered. In order to explain something, you have to first know about it. You learn about it by watching, questioning, and being a student of the Spirit.

Chapter 10: Launch Out Into The Deep

These next few years are going to be full of spiritual adventure. The world, of course, is going to plummet on toward destruction. The church, on the other hand, is going to charge on into glory. In the end time God is going to pour out His Spirit on all flesh and do signs and wonders. We will see displays of God's power in unprecedented ways.

As with any move of the Spirit, there will be excess and counterfeit. There will be those who will go overboard, endorsing and encouraging bizarre and ungodly behavior. There will be some who will turn a blessed experience into a spiritual litmus test and set themselves apart as a spiritual elite. There will be those who will merchandise their gifts and bring reproach to the kingdom. There will be others who, seeing the excess, will declare all supernatural manifestation to be of the devil. But, praise God, there will be those who will steer a good course, clinging to the Word and contending for the supernatural.

There is a wonderful phrase used by the Lord in Luke 5:4. He told Peter to "Launch out into the deep and let down your nets for a catch." There is a big catch coming in the days ahead. To be a part of it requires us to launch out into the deep. This means getting away from the bank and out into the deep water. Getting away from the safe and familiar and being just a little daring. Getting bold enough to obey the Lord when it doesn't make good sense. God has prepared a generation of ministers with a strong grasp on the Word of God. He is now restoring the supernatural flow of the Spirit in an hour when the world is hungry for reality. We must be willing to launch out.

In order for a local church to have a continuous move of supernatural manifestation without becoming spiritually foolish, there must be someone walking in the Gift of Explanation. I am convinced that every pastor can contend for this gift, becoming skilled in discerning, explaining, and directing the flow of the supernatural in every service. The move of the Spirit then becomes light and life to believers, confirming the presence of the Lord in His Church. Eager anticipation builds in a congregation where God is moving supernaturally and yet there is a sense of spiritual stability and safety. Uninformed Christians and unbelievers, instead of labeling the church as insane, will recognize that God is truly in our midst.

Conclusion

This book has been primarily directed toward pastors and other leaders. It can, however, be a blessing to any member of the church who wants to see a consistent move of God in their fellowship. If you are a church member, please do not run to your pastor and try to correct him or instruct him. If you have a close relationship to him you might recommend this book. In any case you can begin to pray for the move of God in the congregation. Paul told us all, as a church, to desire the best gifts. If God wants to change your church He will change it through the Pastor, by the Spirit, in response to the heart-cry of the saints.

If you are a pastor who sees himself in any of the questions or circumstances I have described, take heart. God is no respecter of persons. He wants to flow in your congregation. I am convinced that if you will ask, He will grace you in the Gift of Explanation. As you learn to trust Him, wait on Him, and recognize the gifts in your congregation you will be amazed at the consistent flow of the Spirit, the abiding sense of His Presence in your services. It is a blessing worthy of the effort. Be determined to contend for the supernatural.

About the Author

Virgil and Judy Stokes have served as pastors to congregations in Oklahoma, New York, and Arizona. They are founders of Abundant Heart Ministries, a missionary/evangelistic association training pastors and church leaders at home and abroad. They began developing training programs in 1989 and have continued to expand that ministry.

Faith Ministry Training Institute of Tucson has satellite programs preparing people for ministry at home and abroad. Correspondence courses bring the Word to prisoners and the homebound. Pastor Virgil's ministry focuses on "Building People of Substance for Works of Power," helping churches prepare regular people to do remarkable things. The ministry is marked by a commitment to the truth of the Word of God and the power of the Spirit of God. They are moving people out of the pew and into the harvest.

For additional copies of this book or for a list of all CDs/tapes and books, contact us at:

Abundant Heart Ministry Inc
PO Box 90314
Tucson AZ 85752
e-mail: pastorvirgil@abundantheart.org
www.abundantheart.org

Other Books by the Author

DIAGNOSIS AND TREATMENT OF FOOLS·

The Squeky Wheel Doesn't Have to Get the Grease!

This book will help you recognize problem people and learn to deal with them Biblically. Included are a rating test to find your "Foolishness Quotient" and the characteristics of foolish people. Help keep the fool from stealing your time and peace of mind.

GOD HELP ME I CAN'T STOP!!

A biblical guide for ministry to addicts and alcoholics.

This book combines personal experience, scientific information, and Biblical truth in addressing the problem of addiction. Topics include helping family members, finding treatment alternatives, evaluating support groups, and dealing with the disease concept of addiction. An accompanying workbook and recovery guide, "Principles of Recovery", is also available.

SEVEN PRINCIPLES OF RECOVERY: A WORKBOOK

"Principles" are a piece of practical truth which may be applied in different setting with the same results. "Recovery" is the process of healing and restoration which brings an individual to wholeness. This includes physical and mental healing, repairing of damaged relationships, and a new intimacy with the Creator. This workbook is specifically intended for the individual who thinks he may have a problem with addiction. It will define, discuss, and provide specific instructions and activities that are valid for everyone but absolutely essential to persons in recovery.

Water Baptism

"...believeth and is baptized"

Baptism in water after we are "born again" is basic in becoming a disciple of the Lord Jesus Christ. Jesus says it is part of the disciple-making process; however, it is often an overlooked and underappreciated sideline in many of our churches.

To the early church, believing on the Lord AND being baptized was all one act. How and why have we strayed from this important mandate?

Using history and humor, Rev. Stokes has put together this must-have study of the scriptural background and purpose for water baptism.